THIS BOOK

BELONGS TO

....

....

Did you like my book? I pondered it severely before releasing this book. Although the response has been overwhelming, it is always pleasing to see, read or hear a new comment. Thank you for reading this and I would love to hear your honest opinion about it. Furthermore, many people are searching for a unique book, and your feedback will help me gather the right books for my reading audience.

Thanks!

Copyright @2023

All rights reserved. No part of this publication may be reproduced, stored in a retrieval system, or transmitted in any form or by any means, electronic, mechanical, photocopying, recording or otherwise, without the prior written permission of the Publisher.

Table of Contents

SUMMARY

The Joy of Going Crochet Barefoot with a Twist: This is a comprehensive guidebook that delves into the world of crochet and explores the unique and exciting technique of going barefoot with a twist. This book is perfect for both beginners and experienced crocheters who are looking to expand their skills and create stunning and comfortable footwear.

The author, a seasoned crochet enthusiast, takes readers on a journey through the art of crochet, providing step-by-step instructions and detailed explanations of various stitches and techniques. From the basic chain stitch to more advanced patterns, this book covers it all, ensuring that readers have a solid foundation before diving into the world of barefoot crochet.

What sets this book apart is its focus on the twist technique. The author introduces readers to the concept of adding a twist to their crochet projects, resulting in unique and eye-catching designs. Whether it's a simple twist in the pattern or a more intricate twist in the construction of the footwear, this technique adds a touch of creativity and flair to any crochet project.

This book also includes a wide range of patterns and projects for readers to try. From cozy slippers to stylish sandals, there is something for everyone in this book. Each pattern is accompanied by detailed instructions, clear diagrams, and helpful tips, ensuring that readers can easily follow along and create beautiful footwear.

In addition to the patterns, this book also provides guidance on choosing the right yarn and hook size for each project, as well as tips for customizing the fit and style of the footwear. The author also shares her insights on color selection and embellishments, allowing readers to truly make each project their own.

Beyond the technical aspects, this book also explores the joy and therapeutic benefits of crochet. The author shares personal anecdotes and stories of how crochet has brought her happiness and relaxation, encouraging readers to embrace the craft as a form of self-expression and stress relief.

This book is not just a book about crochet; it is a celebration of creativity, self-care, and the joy of handmade footwear. Whether you're a seasoned crocheter or a complete beginner, this book is sure to inspire and guide you on your crochet journey. So grab your yarn and hook, and get ready to go barefoot with a twist!

Understanding the Appeal of Crochet Barefoot Sandals: Crochet barefoot sandals have gained popularity in recent years due to their unique and appealing design. These sandals are essentially foot jewelry that are made using crochet techniques, resulting in a delicate and intricate pattern that wraps around the foot.

One of the main reasons why crochet barefoot sandals have become so popular is because they offer a stylish and fashionable alternative to traditional sandals. The crochet patterns used in these sandals can be customized to suit individual preferences, allowing for a wide range of designs and styles. This means that individuals can choose a pair of crochet barefoot sandals that perfectly matches their personal style and taste.

Another reason why crochet barefoot sandals are appealing is because they are incredibly versatile. Unlike traditional sandals, which are often limited in terms of design and functionality, crochet barefoot sandals can be worn in a variety of settings and occasions. They can be dressed up or down, making them suitable for both casual and formal events. Additionally, the open design of these sandals allows for breathability, making them perfect for hot summer days or beach outings.

Furthermore, crochet barefoot sandals are also popular because they offer a unique and bohemian aesthetic. The intricate crochet patterns and delicate details add a touch of elegance and femininity to any outfit. They can be paired with a simple sundress or worn with a bikini at the beach, instantly elevating the overall look. The handmade nature of these sandals also adds to their appeal, as they are often seen as a labor of love and craftsmanship.

In addition to their aesthetic appeal, crochet barefoot sandals also offer practical benefits. The crochet material used in these sandals is soft and comfortable, providing a gentle and cushioned feel against the skin. This makes them a great option for individuals who prefer a more natural and barefoot experience, without sacrificing style. Additionally, the adjustable nature of crochet barefoot sandals allows for a perfect fit, ensuring that they stay securely in place while walking or engaging in various activities.

Overall, the appeal of crochet barefoot sandals lies in their unique design, versatility, and aesthetic appeal. These sandals offer a stylish alternative to traditional footwear, allowing individuals to express their personal style and taste. Whether worn for a casual outing or a special occasion, crochet barefoot sandals provide a comfortable and fashionable option that is sure to turn heads.

Gathering Your Crochet Tools and Materials of Crochet Barefoot Sandals:
To successfully gather your crochet tools and materials for making crochet barefoot sandals, you will need to ensure that you have everything you need before starting the project. Crochet barefoot sandals are a fun and trendy accessory that can be worn during the summer months or for beach weddings. They are a great way to add a bohemian touch to your outfit and showcase your crochet skills.

First and foremost, you will need a crochet hook. The size of the hook will depend on the thickness of the yarn you choose to use. It is recommended to use a smaller hook size for a tighter stitch and a larger hook size for a looser stitch. You can refer to the yarn label for guidance on the appropriate hook size to use.

Next, you will need to select the yarn for your project. There are various types of yarn available, such as cotton, acrylic, or bamboo. It is important to choose a yarn that is comfortable to wear and suitable for the purpose of the barefoot sandals. Cotton yarn is a popular choice as it is breathable and soft against the skin. You can choose a single color or opt for a variegated yarn to add visual interest to your sandals.

In addition to the crochet hook and yarn, you will also need a pair of scissors. These will be used to cut the yarn when necessary and trim any loose ends. It is important to have a sharp pair of scissors to ensure clean cuts and prevent fraying of the yarn.

To keep track of your progress and count stitches, it is helpful to have stitch markers. These can be small plastic rings or even safety pins that can be inserted into the stitches to mark specific points in your pattern. Stitch markers are especially useful when working on complex patterns or when you need to keep track of increases or decreases.

Another essential tool for crocheting barefoot sandals is a tapestry needle. This needle is used for weaving in loose ends and sewing any necessary seams. It is important to choose a tapestry needle with a large eye to accommodate the thickness of the yarn you are using.

Lastly, you may want to consider having a crochet pattern or tutorial on hand. This will guide you through the process of creating the barefoot sandals and ensure that you are following the correct stitch pattern and measurements. There are many free patterns available online, or you can purchase a pattern book specifically for crochet accessories.

Crochet Stitches Used in Barefoot Sandals: Barefoot sandals are a popular accessory for those who want to add a touch of bohemian style to their summer outfits. These unique sandals are designed to be worn without shoes, allowing the wearer to feel the sand beneath their feet while still looking fashionable. One of the key elements in creating barefoot sandals is the use of crochet stitches.

Crochet is a versatile craft that involves creating fabric by interlocking loops of yarn or thread using a crochet hook. There are several different crochet stitches that can be used to create the intricate patterns and designs found in barefoot sandals.

One of the most commonly used crochet stitches in barefoot sandals is the chain stitch. This stitch is the foundation for many crochet projects and is used to create a base row or foundation chain. It is a simple stitch that involves pulling a loop of yarn through another loop to create a chain. The chain stitch is often used to create the straps or ties that hold the barefoot sandals in place.

Another popular crochet stitch used in barefoot sandals is the single crochet stitch. This stitch is worked by inserting the crochet hook into a stitch, yarn over, and pulling through both loops on the hook. The single crochet stitch creates a dense and sturdy fabric, making it ideal for creating the soles or bottoms of the barefoot sandals.

The double crochet stitch is another commonly used stitch in barefoot sandals. This stitch is worked by yarn over, inserting the hook into a stitch, yarn over again, and pulling through the first two loops on the hook. Then, yarn over again and pull through the remaining two loops on the hook. The double crochet stitch creates a taller and more open fabric, making it perfect for creating decorative elements or lace-like patterns in the barefoot sandals.

In addition to these basic crochet stitches, there are also more advanced stitches that can be used to create intricate designs in barefoot sandals. These include the treble crochet stitch, which is worked by yarn over twice before inserting the hook into a stitch, and the half double crochet stitch, which is worked by yarn over, inserting the hook into a stitch, yarn over again, and pulling through all three loops on the hook.

Overall, the use of crochet stitches in barefoot sandals allows for endless possibilities in terms of design and style. Whether you prefer a simple and minimalist look or a more intricate and detailed design, crochet stitches can be used to create the perfect pair of barefoot sandals to suit your personal style.

Tips for Choosing the Right Yarn and Hook of Crochet Barefoot Sandals:
When it comes to choosing the right yarn and hook for crochet barefoot sandals, there are a few factors to consider. The yarn and hook you choose will greatly impact the final look and feel of your sandals, so it's important to make the right choices.

Firstly, let's talk about yarn. When selecting yarn for crochet barefoot sandals, you'll want to consider the weight, fiber content, and color. The weight of the yarn refers to its thickness, and it can range from super fine to super bulky. For barefoot sandals, you'll generally want to choose a lightweight yarn that is comfortable to wear and won't feel too heavy on your feet. A yarn with a weight of 1 or 2 is usually a good choice.

Next, consider the fiber content of the yarn. Different fibers have different properties, so think about what you want from your barefoot sandals. If you're looking for a soft and comfortable feel, natural fibers like cotton or bamboo are great options. These fibers are breathable and will keep your feet cool in warm weather. If you're looking for durability, synthetic fibers like acrylic or nylon may be a better choice. These fibers are often more resistant to wear and tear.

Color is another important consideration when choosing yarn for barefoot sandals. Think about the overall look you want to achieve. Do you want your sandals to be bright and colorful, or do you prefer a more neutral and understated look? Consider the colors that will complement your skin tone and the outfits you plan to wear with the sandals.

Now let's move on to hooks. The size of the hook you choose will determine the size of the stitches and the overall gauge of your crochet work. For barefoot sandals, you'll generally want to use a smaller hook size to create a tighter stitch and a more delicate look. A hook size between 2.25mm and 3.5mm is often a good choice for barefoot sandals.

However, it's important to note that the hook size you choose should also be compatible with the yarn you've selected. Most yarn labels will provide a recommended hook size range for that particular yarn. Make sure to check this information and choose a hook size that falls within the recommended range.

In addition to the size, consider the material of the hook. Crochet hooks can be made from various materials such as aluminum, plastic, or wood.

How to Read Crochet Patterns and Diagrams of Crochet Barefoot Sandals: Crochet patterns and diagrams are essential tools for anyone interested in creating beautiful and intricate crochet projects, such as barefoot sandals. Whether you are a beginner or an experienced crocheter, understanding how to read these patterns and diagrams is crucial for successfully completing your project.

To start, it is important to familiarize yourself with the basic symbols and abbreviations commonly used in crochet patterns. These symbols represent different stitches and techniques that you will need to know in order to follow the pattern correctly. Some common symbols include a chain stitch (represented by a small "v" shape), a single crochet stitch (represented by a small "x" shape), and a double crochet stitch (represented by a taller "x" shape). By understanding these symbols, you will be able to decipher the instructions provided in the pattern.

In addition to symbols, crochet patterns also use abbreviations to save space and make the instructions more concise. Some common abbreviations include "ch" for chain, "sc" for single crochet, and "dc" for double crochet. It is important to refer to the pattern's key or legend to understand the meaning of each abbreviation used. This will help you follow the pattern accurately and avoid any confusion.

Once you have familiarized yourself with the symbols and abbreviations, it is time to move on to reading the actual pattern instructions. Crochet patterns are typically written in a step-by-step format, guiding you through each stitch and technique required to complete the project. It is important to read the pattern carefully and understand each instruction before moving on to the next step. Take your time and refer back to the symbols and abbreviations as needed to ensure you are following the pattern correctly.

In addition to written instructions, crochet patterns often include diagrams or charts to provide a visual representation of the pattern. These diagrams use symbols and lines to illustrate the stitches and their placement. While some crocheters may find diagrams more intuitive to follow, others may prefer written instructions. It is important to choose the format that works best for you and practice reading both patterns and diagrams to become comfortable with both methods.

When it comes to crocheting barefoot sandals, understanding how to read patterns and diagrams is especially important. These intricate designs often involve various stitches and techniques that may be new to some crocheters. By carefully studying the pattern and referring to the symbols and abbreviations, you will be able to create stunning barefoot sandals that are both stylish and comfortable.

Customizing Fit for Different Foot Sizes of Crochet Barefoot Sandals:
When it comes to crochet barefoot sandals, one size does not fit all. Each individual has unique foot sizes and shapes, and it is essential to customize the fit to ensure maximum comfort and functionality. By tailoring the sandals to different foot sizes, we can provide a personalized experience for our customers, allowing them to enjoy the freedom of going barefoot while still having the support and protection they need.

To achieve a customized fit, several factors need to be considered. First and foremost, the length of the sandals should be adjusted to match the wearer's foot size. This can be done by either adding or subtracting rows in the crochet pattern, depending on whether the foot is larger or smaller than the standard size. By doing so, we can ensure that the sandals fit snugly without being too tight or loose.

In addition to length, the width of the sandals also plays a crucial role in achieving a comfortable fit. Some individuals may have wider or narrower feet, and it is important to accommodate these variations. This can be achieved by adjusting the number of stitches in the pattern or incorporating additional increases or decreases in specific areas of the sandals. By customizing the width, we can prevent any discomfort or rubbing that may occur if the sandals are too tight or too loose.

Furthermore, the shape of the foot should also be taken into consideration. Some individuals may have high arches or flat feet, which can affect the way the sandals fit and provide support. By incorporating specific design elements, such as arch support or extra padding, we can cater to these unique foot shapes and ensure that the sandals provide the necessary comfort and stability.

Another aspect to consider when customizing the fit is the fastening mechanism of the sandals. While some individuals may prefer a simple tie-up design, others may require a more secure closure, such as a buckle or Velcro strap. By offering different options for fastening, we can accommodate various foot sizes and preferences, ensuring that the sandals stay in place during wear.

Lastly, it is important to communicate with our customers and gather their specific foot measurements to ensure the best possible fit. This can be done through a simple questionnaire or by providing guidelines on how to measure their feet accurately. By collecting this information, we can create a truly customized experience for each individual, taking into account their unique foot size, shape, and preferences.

In conclusion, customizing the fit for different foot sizes of crochet barefoot sandals is essential to provide maximum comfort and functionality.

Adding Unique Touches with Embellishments of Crochet Barefoot Sandals: Adding unique touches to your style can be easily achieved with the use of embellishments, and one way to do this is by incorporating crochet barefoot sandals into your wardrobe. These delicate and intricate accessories not only add a touch of elegance to your overall look, but they also provide a unique and eye-catching element that sets you apart from the crowd.

Crochet barefoot sandals are essentially foot jewelry that are designed to be worn without shoes, making them perfect for beach weddings, music festivals, or simply for adding a bohemian flair to your everyday outfits. They are typically made using a crochet hook and various types of yarn or thread, allowing for endless possibilities when it comes to color, texture, and design.

One of the main advantages of crochet barefoot sandals is their versatility. They can be customized to match any outfit or occasion, whether you prefer a simple and understated design or a more elaborate and intricate pattern. You can choose to incorporate beads, sequins, or even feathers into your crochet work, adding a touch of glamour and sophistication to your feet.

Furthermore, crochet barefoot sandals are not only aesthetically pleasing, but they also serve a practical purpose. They provide a layer of protection for your feet, preventing them from coming into direct contact with hot sand, rough surfaces, or sharp objects. This makes them a great alternative to traditional sandals or flip-flops, especially in warmer climates or during outdoor activities.

In addition to their practicality, crochet barefoot sandals also offer a sense of freedom and comfort. Unlike traditional shoes, they allow your feet to breathe and move naturally, giving you a barefoot sensation while still providing a stylish and fashionable look. This makes them a popular choice among those who value both style and comfort.

When it comes to styling crochet barefoot sandals, the possibilities are endless. They can be paired with a flowy maxi dress for a bohemian-inspired look, or with a bikini and cover-up for a beach-ready ensemble. They can also be worn with shorts, skirts, or even jeans to add a unique and unexpected twist to your everyday outfits.

In conclusion, crochet barefoot sandals are a fantastic way to add unique touches and embellishments to your style. With their delicate crochet work, customizable designs, and practicality, they offer a versatile and fashionable accessory that can elevate any outfit. So why not give your feet the attention they deserve and embrace the beauty of crochet barefoot sandals?

Adapting Patterns for Children and Men of Crochet Barefoot Sandals: Adapting patterns for children and men of crochet barefoot sandals involves making modifications to the existing patterns to ensure a comfortable and proper fit for individuals of different sizes and foot shapes.

When it comes to children, it is important to consider their smaller foot size and the fact that their feet are still growing. This means that the pattern needs to be adjusted to accommodate their specific measurements. The length and width of the sandals may need to be reduced, and the straps may need to be made shorter to fit their smaller feet. Additionally, the pattern may need to be simplified to make it easier for children to follow and complete the project.

For men, the main consideration is their larger foot size and the need for a more masculine design. The pattern may need to be enlarged to fit their feet comfortably, and the straps may need to be made longer to accommodate their wider feet. The design of the sandals may also need to be adjusted to have a more rugged and masculine appearance, using thicker yarn or incorporating different stitch patterns.

In both cases, it is important to keep in mind the comfort and functionality of the sandals. The pattern should be adapted to ensure that the sandals stay securely on the feet without causing any discomfort or irritation. This may involve making adjustments to the strap placement or adding additional support to the sole of the sandals.

Furthermore, it is essential to consider the skill level of the crocheter when adapting patterns for children and men. The instructions should be clear and easy to follow, especially for beginners. Providing detailed explanations and step-by-step photos or diagrams can greatly assist in ensuring that the pattern is accessible to crocheters of all skill levels.

Overall, adapting patterns for children and men of crochet barefoot sandals requires careful consideration of their specific needs and preferences. By making the necessary modifications to the pattern, it is possible to create comfortable and stylish sandals that are suitable for individuals of all ages and genders.

Proper Finishing Techniques for Durability of Crochet Barefoot Sandals: Proper finishing techniques are essential for ensuring the durability of crochet barefoot sandals. These finishing techniques not only enhance the overall appearance of the sandals but also help to prevent them from unraveling or coming apart over time.

One important finishing technique is weaving in the loose ends of yarn. When crocheting barefoot sandals, there are often multiple yarn ends that need to be secured. These loose ends can be woven into the stitches of the sandal using a yarn needle. By weaving in the ends, the yarn is locked in place, preventing it from unraveling or becoming loose with wear. This technique also creates a neater and more professional-looking finish.

Another important finishing technique is blocking the finished sandals. Blocking involves shaping and stretching the crochet piece to its desired size and shape. For barefoot sandals, blocking helps to ensure that they fit comfortably and securely on the foot. Blocking can be done by wetting the sandals and then pinning them to a blocking board or surface, allowing them to dry in the desired shape. This technique helps to set the stitches and prevent them from stretching or distorting over time.

Additionally, adding a border or edging to the barefoot sandals can help to reinforce the edges and prevent them from fraying or unraveling. A simple single crochet or slip stitch border can be worked around the edges of the sandals to provide a clean and finished look. This border not only adds to the overall durability of the sandals but also helps to prevent the stitches from coming undone.

Furthermore, using a strong and durable yarn is crucial for the longevity of crochet barefoot sandals. Choosing a yarn that is specifically designed for footwear or that has a high percentage of natural fibers, such as cotton or bamboo, can help to ensure that the sandals withstand regular wear and tear. These types of yarns are less likely to stretch or break, making them ideal for creating durable and long-lasting barefoot sandals.

In conclusion, proper finishing techniques are essential for ensuring the durability of crochet barefoot sandals. Weaving in loose ends, blocking the finished piece, adding a border or edging, and using a strong and durable yarn all contribute to the overall longevity and quality of the sandals. By following these techniques, crocheters can create barefoot sandals that not only look beautiful but also withstand the test of time.

Washing and Caring for Your Crochet Barefoot Sandals: Washing and caring for your crochet barefoot sandals is essential to maintain their quality and prolong their lifespan. These delicate accessories require special attention to ensure they remain clean, fresh, and in good condition. By following a few simple steps, you can keep your crochet barefoot sandals looking beautiful and ready to wear.

Firstly, it is important to note that crochet barefoot sandals are typically made from delicate materials such as cotton or acrylic yarn. Therefore, it is recommended to hand wash them instead of using a washing machine. Fill a basin or sink with lukewarm water and add a mild detergent specifically designed for delicate fabrics. Avoid using harsh chemicals or bleach, as they can damage the fibers and cause discoloration.

Gently submerge the crochet barefoot sandals in the soapy water and swish them around to ensure they are fully immersed. Allow them to soak for a few minutes to loosen any dirt or debris. Then, using your hands, gently rub the sandals to remove any stains or dirt. Be careful not to pull or stretch the crochet stitches, as this can cause them to unravel or lose their shape.

Once you have cleaned the sandals, rinse them thoroughly under cool running water to remove any soap residue. Make sure to squeeze out excess water gently, avoiding any twisting or wringing motions that can damage the delicate crochet work. It is best to lay the sandals flat on a clean towel and roll them up to absorb the remaining moisture. Avoid hanging them to dry, as this can cause them to stretch or lose their shape.

After the crochet barefoot sandals are mostly dry, reshape them gently with your hands to ensure they retain their original design. Lay them flat on a clean, dry towel or a mesh drying rack, allowing them to air dry completely. Avoid exposing them to direct sunlight or heat sources, as this can cause fading or shrinkage.

In terms of storage, it is recommended to keep your crochet barefoot sandals in a cool, dry place away from direct sunlight. Avoid folding or creasing them, as this can create permanent lines or wrinkles. If you want to protect them further, you can store them in a breathable fabric bag or wrap them in acid-free tissue paper.

In summary, washing and caring for your crochet barefoot sandals involves gentle hand washing with a mild detergent, thorough rinsing, and careful drying to maintain their quality and shape. By following these steps and storing them properly, you can enjoy your crochet barefoot sandals for many seasons to come.

Storage Tips to Keep Them Looking Great of Crochet Barefoot Sandals: Crochet barefoot sandals are a trendy and fashionable accessory that can add a unique touch to any summer outfit. However, like any other delicate item, they require proper care and storage to keep them looking great and ensure their longevity. Here are some storage tips to help you maintain the beauty and quality of your crochet barefoot sandals:

1. Clean and dry: Before storing your crochet barefoot sandals, make sure they are clean and completely dry. Any dirt or moisture left on the sandals can lead to mold or mildew growth, which can damage the delicate crochet work. Gently hand wash the sandals using a mild detergent and lukewarm water, and then allow them to air dry completely.

2. Avoid direct sunlight: Crochet materials are often sensitive to sunlight, as prolonged exposure can cause fading or discoloration. Therefore, it is important to store your barefoot sandals in a cool and dark place, away from direct sunlight. Consider using a storage box or a fabric bag to protect them from any potential light exposure.

3. Use acid-free tissue paper: To maintain the shape and structure of your crochet barefoot sandals, stuff them with acid-free tissue paper. This will help prevent any creasing or folding that may occur during storage. Avoid using regular tissue paper, as it may contain acids that can damage the delicate fibers of the crochet work.

4. Store in a breathable container: It is essential to store your crochet barefoot sandals in a breathable container to prevent any moisture buildup. Avoid using plastic bags or airtight containers, as they can trap moisture and lead to mold growth. Instead, opt for a fabric bag or a shoebox with ventilation holes to allow air circulation.

5. Separate and organize: If you own multiple pairs of crochet barefoot sandals, it is advisable to store them separately to avoid any tangling or damage.

Consider using individual fabric bags or compartments within a storage box to keep each pair organized and protected.

6. Avoid hanging: While it may be tempting to hang your crochet barefoot sandals, it is not recommended. Hanging can cause the sandals to stretch or lose their shape over time. Instead, lay them flat in the storage container, ensuring they are not folded or pressed against any sharp objects.

Sharing Your Creations with the World of Crochet Barefoot Sandals: When it comes to the world of crochet, there are endless possibilities for creating unique and beautiful items. One such item that has gained popularity in recent years is the crochet barefoot sandal. These delicate and intricate creations are not only a stylish accessory for the beach or summer festivals, but they also showcase the skill and creativity of the crocheter.

If you have mastered the art of crochet and have created your own barefoot sandals, you may be wondering how to share your creations with the world. There are several avenues you can explore to showcase your work and potentially even turn your hobby into a business.

One of the most popular ways to share your crochet creations is through social media platforms such as Instagram, Facebook, and Pinterest. These platforms allow you to create a visual portfolio of your work, where you can showcase your barefoot sandals in various settings and styles. By using hashtags and engaging with the crochet community, you can attract a following of fellow crochet enthusiasts who appreciate your talent and may even be interested in purchasing your creations.

Another option is to create your own website or online store. This gives you complete control over how your barefoot sandals are presented and allows you to reach a wider audience. You can include high-quality photographs of your creations, detailed descriptions, and even offer customization options for your customers. Additionally, having your own website or online store gives you the opportunity to build your brand and establish yourself as a reputable crochet artist.

If you prefer a more hands-on approach, you can also consider selling your barefoot sandals at local craft fairs, markets, or even through consignment in boutiques or specialty stores. This allows you to interact directly with potential customers, answer any questions they may have, and receive immediate feedback on your creations. It also provides an opportunity to network with other artisans and potentially collaborate on future projects.

In addition to sharing your creations through various platforms, it is important to continuously improve your skills and stay up-to-date with the latest crochet trends. Attend workshops, take online courses, and join crochet communities to learn new techniques and gain inspiration from other talented crocheters. By constantly challenging yourself and pushing the boundaries of your creativity, you can ensure that your barefoot sandals remain fresh and appealing to your audience.

Sharing your crochet barefoot sandals with the world is not only a way to showcase your talent and passion, but it also allows you to connect with a community of like-minded individuals who appreciate the art of crochet.

Introduction

Make your feet happy...

Look at those poor neglected toes. They deserve to be adorned with the latest crochet accessory: beautiful barefoot sandals.

Happy feet mean happy you, and with the perfect accessory for summer you won't be able to resist skipping lightly through lush grass, feeling the beach beneath your feet, or rocking that Ibiza hot spot. With eight designs to choose from you can create stunning foot couture to match any occasion. Grace a beach wedding with delicate Ivory Star Flowers, display your festival chic with the Ferris Wheel Mandala design, or flaunt your flower power with a dainty Daisy Chain. Each pattern is small in scale and quick to make, so there's no need to stop at just one pair.

Remember that with all these little beauties you can add your unique stamp by choosing colours that match your outfit, your mood or your yarn stash. Because they really don't take much yarn to make, barefoot sandals are the perfect way to use up half balls and leftover bits and pieces.

If you need a little help with any of the stitches, take a look at the instructions at the very end of the book. There you will find all you need to get you hooking with success. And if you love these designs you can visit the blogs of the talented designers that created them. So explore and discover a whole new way to crochet for your feet.

Never mind socks – this is what the beautiful and creative crocheter is making!

Daisy Chain

I remember endless summer days spent running around barefoot on lush green grass studded with daisies, before finally getting on with the serious business of the day: making a daisy chain to adorn my hair, one for my wrist and another for my ankle. These days my chains are of the crochet kind so I have hooked up this daisy pattern to go with them.

You will need

- 4 ply cotton yarn, one ball each in three colours. I used Patons cotton 4 ply in apple 01205 (A), yellow 01740 (B) and white 01691 (C)
- Crochet hook: 2mm
- Yarn needle and scissors
- Steam iron

Stitches used

- ✓ Chain (ch)
- ✓ Double crochet (dc)
- ✓ Half treble (htr)
- ✓ Treble crochet (tr)
- ✓ Slip stitch (sl st)
- ✓ Picot stitch (picot)

Ankle ties and leaves

make 2

Leaf 1

With colour A, make 7 chain. Turn, and starting in 2nd ch from hook work one st in each ch as follows: dc, htr, htr, tr, htr, dc.

Work 3ch and sl st in 3rd ch from hook to make picot. Turn so that you are ready to work along the back loops of the initial chain and work one st in each of the back loops as follows: dc, htr, tr, htr, htr, dc. Sl st to join and do not fasten off.

Ankle tie

Continue to ch until your chain equals 120cm (48in) in length. Do not fasten off.

Leaf 2

Make 10 chain, sl st in 3rd ch from hook to make picot, then starting in next ch work one st in each ch as follows: dc, htr, tr, htr, htr, dc, 1ch.

Now work along the back loops of the initial chain and work one st in each of the back loops as follows: dc, htr, htr, tr, htr, dc, sl st to join. Fasten off.

Daisy Motif

make 6

Round 1: With colour B make 4 chain. Work the following into 4th ch from hook: tr, 1ch, (trcl, 1ch) 6 times, sl st to top of first tr and fasten off. (7 trcl [1 is made from 4ch and tr], 7 ch-sps)

Round 2: Join colour C in next ch-sp, (4ch, 2ttr, 4ch, sl st) in each ch-sp around, sl st to beg ch-sp. Fasten off and weave in ends.

TIP
Make these daisies in in other colours, perhaps yellow petals and brown centres to suggest sunflowers, or anything else that matches you mood or outfit.

Making up

Sew in all ends.

Set your iron to steam. Steam press the back of each motif and the leaves of the chain strap to flatten them out and neaten them up.

Double over an ankle tie. Using a length of colour B and the yarn needle, attach three daisy motifs at 6cm intervals along the tie, starting about 6cm down from the loop. Stitch only the back and the centre of each motif, making sure to catch through both strands of the colour A tie rather than just sewing over it otherwise the motifs will slide off. Repeat for the second sandal.

Ferris Wheel Mandala

One of my favourite summer outings is a trip to the fair. I like to let all the whirling sounds, colours and lights engulf me and carry me away for a day of fun. The circular motifs for these sandals remind me of the bright lights of the ferris wheel which may be glimpsed in the distance when the fair is in town.

You will need

- 4 ply cotton yarn, one ball each in five colours. I used Patons cotton 4 ply in jade 01726 (A), yellow 01740 (B), purple 01743 (C), nectarine 01723 (D) and raffia 01714 (E)
- Crochet hook: 2mm
- Yarn needle and scissors
- Steam iron

Stitches used

- ✓ Chain (ch)
- ✓ Double crochet (dc)
- ✓ Treble crochet (tr)
- ✓ Triple Treble (ttr)
- ✓ Slip stitch (sl st)

Mandala motif

make 2

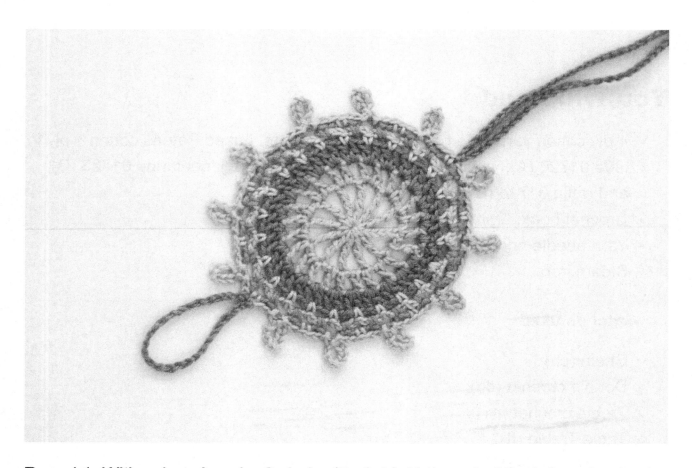

Round 1: With colour A make 8 chain. (ttr, 2ch) 11 times in 8th ch from hook, sl st to 6th ch of initial ch8. Fasten off. (12 ttr, 12 ch-sp)

Round 2: Join colour B in next ch-sp and work 5ch. (tr, 2ch) in each ttr and each ch-sp around and fasten off. (24 tr, 24 ch-sp)

Round 3: Join colour C in next ch-sp and work 4ch, tr in the same ch-sp. (tr, 1ch, tr) in each remaining ch-sp around, ss to 3rd ch of initial ch4 and fasten off. (24 clusters of 2 tr)

Round 4: Join colour D in next ch-sp and work 4ch. (dc in next ch-sp, 3ch) around, ss in 1st ch of beg ch4 and fasten off. (24dc, 24 ch-sp)

Round 5: Join colour E in next ch-sp and work 4ch. (dc in next ch-sp, 3ch) around, ss in 1st ch of beg ch4 and fasten off. (24dc, 24 ch-sp)

Round 6: Join colour A in next ch-sp. *8ch, ss in 8th ch from hook, ss in same ch-sp, 2ch, dc in next ch-sp, 2ch, ss in next ch-sp,* Repeat around to last ch-sp, ss in 1st ch of beg ch8 and fasten off.

Sew in all ends.

Set your iron to steam. Steam press the back of both motifs to flatten them out and neaten them up.

TIP

When sewing in the yarn ends try to weave each colour into a same colour stitch to keep the motif tidy on the back as well as the front.

Toe loop and ankle ties

Add a toe loop and ankle ties to each mandala to complete the sandals, as follows:

Toe loop

make 2

Join colour C in any dc of last round of mandala. Ch 28, ss to same dc to make a loop and fasten off.

Ankle ties

make 2 pairs

Join colour C in opposite dc of mandala to toe loop and chain until the ankle tie is 72cm (28in) in length. Then make another 8ch and ss in 8th ch from hook to make loop. Fasten off and sew in ends. Rejoin colour C in same dc and repeat to make second ankle tie.

Ibiza Triangles

This shade of emerald blue always makes me think of the warm waves of the Mediterranean. These sandals could be made in any colour, as long as wearing them whisks you away to balmy beaches and hot night spots, if only in your imagination!

You will need

- Cotton lurex yarn, one ball. I used Rico Essentials Cotton Lurex, in emerald 010
- Crochet hook: 2.5mm (US B/1)
- Yarn needle and scissors

Stitches used

- ✓ Chain (ch)
- ✓ Double crochet (dc)
- ✓ Half treble crochet (htr)
- ✓ Treble crochet (tr)
- ✓ Slip stitch (sl st)
- ✓ Picot stitch (picot)

Ibiza triangles motif

make 2

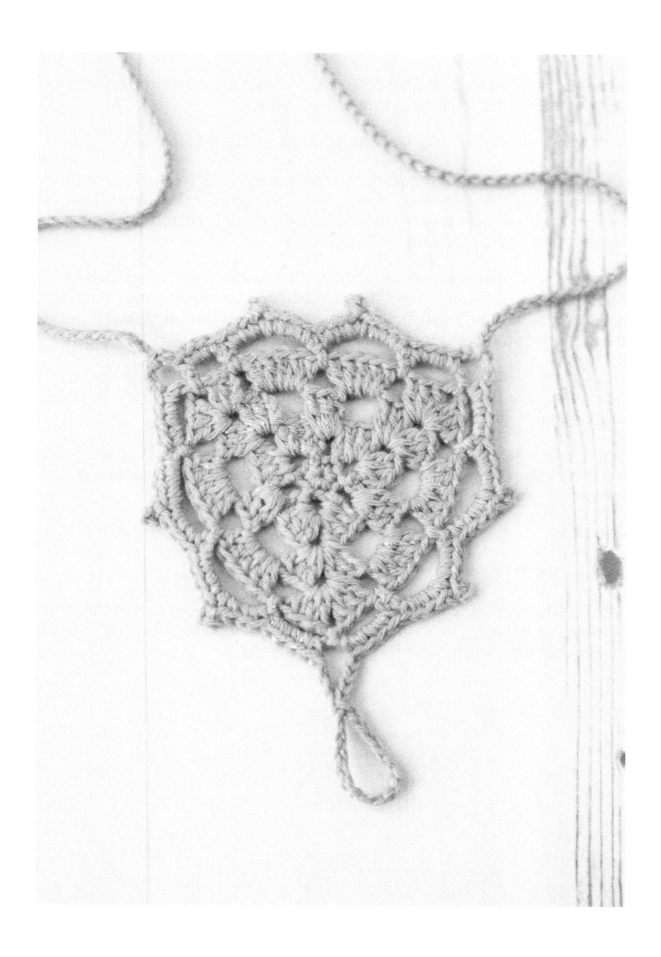

Round 1: Either work 6dc into a magic ring or make 2 chain and work 6dc in 2nd chain from hook. Sl st to first dc to join round. (6dc)

Round 2: 5ch, sl st in next dc. Repeat around to make 6 loops.

Round 3: Sl st into ch5-sp and work 3ch (counts as tr), 2tr, 2ch, 3tr in same space. 1ch, then sl st into next ch5-sp, 1ch. *(3tr, 2ch, 3tr) in next ch5-sp, 1ch, sl st in next ch5-sp, 1ch* repeat from * to * once more. Sl st to top of initial ch3 to join round. (3 corners made up of 3tr, 2ch, 3tr)

Round 4: Sl st around to first ch2-sp and then sl st into this ch2-sp. 3ch (counts as tr), 2tr, 2ch, 3tr in same space, 4ch, 3tr in space between corner clusters, *4ch, (3tr, 2ch, 3tr in ch2-sp), 4ch*, 3tr in next space between clusters*, repeat from * to * once more, sl st to top of ch3 to join round.

Round 5: Sl st into ch2-sp. (3ch (counts as tr), 2tr, 2ch, 3tr in same space), 1ch (5tr in ch4-sp, 1ch, x2), *(3tr, 2ch, 3tr in ch5-sp), 1ch, (5tr in ch4-sp, 1ch, x2)* repeat around. Sl st to top of ch3 to join round.

Round 6: Sl st into ch2-sp, 5ch, sl st in ch1-sp, (7ch, sl st in ch1-sp x2), *(5ch, sl st in ch1-sp x2), (7ch, sl st in ch1-sp x2)* repeat around. 5ch, sl st in ch1-sp to join round.

Fasten off.

Attach new piece of yarn and begin at ch7-sp.

Round 7: (4dc, picot, 4dc in ch7-sp x2), 4dc in ch5-sp, 19ch, sl st in 15th ch from hook to create toe-loop, 4ch, 4dc in next ch5-sp, *4dc, picot, 4dc in ch7-sp x2), 4dc in ch5-sp, 4ch, 4dc in next ch5-sp* repeat around.

Fasten off and weave in ends.

Block your motifs to neaten them by damping with warm water and pinning into shape until dry.

Ankle ties

make 2 pairs

Sl st in ch-4 sp, 150ch, 1tr in 4th ch from hook, 1tr, 1htr, 1dc, sl st.

Fasten off, weave in ends.

Under the Sea

by Anna Fazakerley

I love the beach and swimming in the sea. The colours of the water in the summer sunshine are beautiful. These sandals are designed to look like little fishes swimming over your feet through the waves of the ocean. Set with glistening glass beads they will shimmer around your ankles for added glamour.

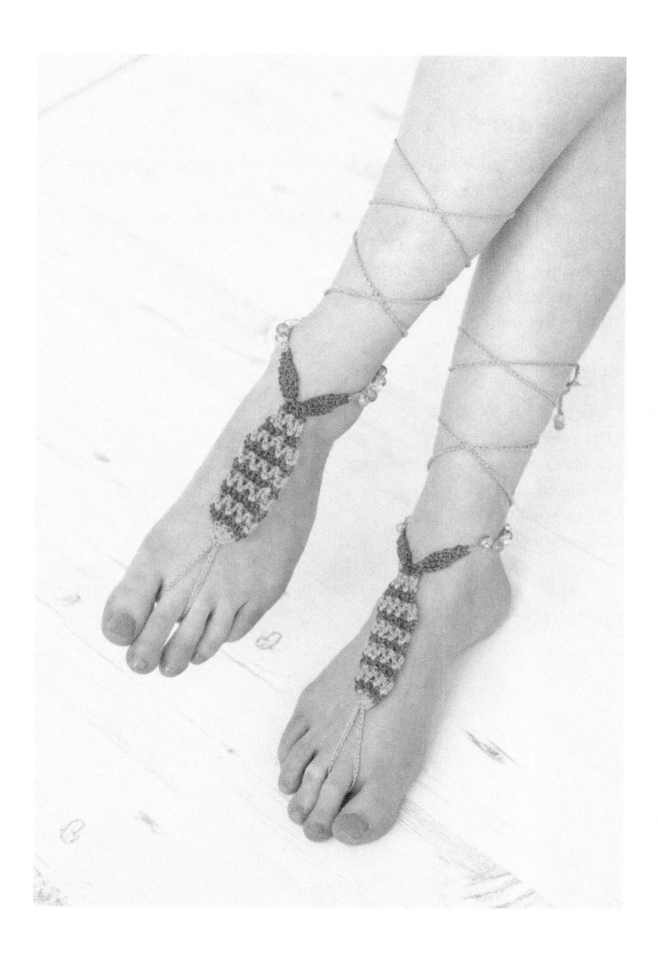

You will need

- 4 ply cotton yarn in two colours. I used Patons cotton 4 ply in jade 01726 (A) and delta 01729 (B)
- 24 glass beads with a large enough hole for the 4 ply yarn to pull through
- Crochet hook: 2mm
- Beading needle
- Yarn needle and scissors
- Steam iron

Stitches used

- ✓ Chain (ch)
- ✓ Double crochet (dc)
- ✓ Double crochet two together (dc2tog)
- ✓ Treble crochet (tr)
- ✓ Triple Treble (ttr)
- ✓ Slip stitch (sl st)

Fish motif

make 2

With colour A, ch28 and sl st in 1st chain to make a loop. Do not fasten off. Turn and continue to work in rows facing away from the chain loop.

Row 1: (3ch, 6tr) in 1st chain of loop. Do not turn, fasten off. (7 tr)

Row 2: Join colour B in top of initial ch3 from previous row. 4ch, tr, miss 1tr, (tr, 1ch, tr, miss 1 tr) to end, do not turn, fasten off. (8 tr, 4 ch-sp)

Row 3: Join colour A in 1st ch-sp. 4ch, tr into same ch-sp. Then work (tr, 1ch, tr) into next three ch-sps to end. Do not turn, fasten off. (8 tr, 4 ch-sp)

Row 4: Join colour B in 1st ch-sp, 4ch, tr into same ch-sp. Then work (tr, 1ch, tr) into next three ch-sps to end. Do not turn, fasten off. (8 tr, 4 ch-sp)

Rows 5–8: Repeat rows 3–4.

Row 9: Repeat row 3.

Row 10: Join colour B in 1st ch-sp and work 3ch. (tr, 1ch, tr) in next 2 ch-sps, tr in last ch-sp, do not turn, fasten off. (6tr, 2 ch-sp)

Row 11: Join colour A in top of 3ch and work 3ch. (tr, 1ch, tr) in next 2 ch-sps, tr in last tr, do not turn, fasten off. (6tr, 2 ch-sp)

Row 12: Join colour B in top of 3ch and work 3ch, tr in next 2 ch-sps, tr in final tr, turn, do not fasten off. (4tr)

Right-hand fin

Row 13: 5ch, 3ttr in same tr, turn, do not fasten off.

Row 14: 3ch, tr in next 3 st, turn, do not fasten off.

Row 15: 1ch, dc2tog, dc in last st, turn, do not fasten off.

Row 16: 5ch, sl st in last st and fasten off.

Left-hand fin

Row 13: Rejoin colour B on WS in last st on the right hand side, work 5ch, 3ttr in same tr, turn, do not fasten off.

Row 14: 3ch, tr in next 3 st, turn, do not fasten off.

Row 15: 1ch, dc2tog, dc in last st, turn, do not fasten off.

Row 16: 5ch, sl st in last st, fasten off.

Ankle ties

make 2 pairs
Thread 24 beads onto colour A yarn ready to use.

Join colour A in the ch-sp on the first tail fin. (2ch, ch over bead), until 9 beads have been added. Continue to chain until the ankle tie is 72cm (28in) in length, then work 2ch, ch over bead until 3 more beads have been added. Fasten off and sew in ends. Rejoin colour B in ch-sp on other fin and repeat to make the second length of ankle tie.

Making up

Sew in all ends.

Set your iron to steam. Steam press the back of both motifs to flatten them out and neaten them up.

Add ankle ties to the ends of the fins and work in the beads to finish.

> **TIP**
> Don't skip the steam pressing of your fish motifs. The sandals will curl and not fit as neatly on your foot.

Flower Trio

designed Cara Medus

These sandals, as the name suggests, are made from three pretty flowers that will bloom on your feet, starting with the large one at the top. Hook yourself a cascade of petalled perfection that's ideal for a day relaxing in the garden.

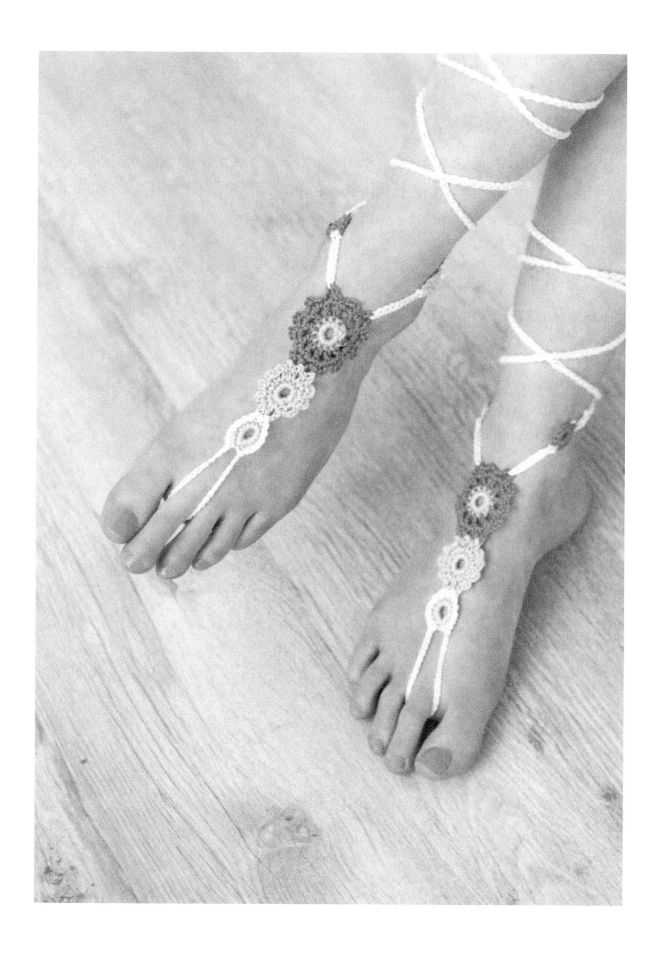

You will need

- Mercerized long-staple cotton yarn, one ball each in three colours. I used DMC Petra 3 in cream 54459 (A), light pink 53326 (B) and dark pink 53805 (C)
- Crochet hooks: 3mm and 4mm (US 6)
- Yarn needle and scissors

Stitches used

✓ Chain (ch)
✓ Double crochet (dc)
✓ Treble crochet (tr)
✓ Slip stitch (sl st)

Sandal motifs

make 2

Note that each motif is joined to the next as you work the last round. The toe loop forms part of the last round of the third, smallest, motif.

Large flower motif

With colour B and 3mm hook make 6 chain and sl st to first ch to join into a ring.

Round 1 (RS): Ch1 (does not count as st), 12dc into ring, sl st to first dc to join, fasten off. (12 dc)

Round 2: Join colour C in any st with a sl st, ch4 (counts as tr and ch1). Tr, ch1 in the next st, then (tr, ch1) in each st around. Sl st to third ch of beg ch-4. (12 tr, 12 ch- sps)

Round 3: Sl st into first ch-1 sp, ch1 (does not count as st), then work (dc, ch3, dc) into the same ch-sp and then in each ch-sp around. Sl st to first dc and fasten off.

Medium flower motif

With colour B and 3mm hook make 6 chain and sl st to first ch to join into a ring.

Round 1 (RS): Ch1 (does not count as st), 12dc into ring, sl st to first dc to join. (12 dc)

Round 2: Ch1 (does not count as st), (dc in next st, ch3) 9 times, *dc in next st, ch1, sl st in any ch-3 sp on outside of large flower motif, inserting hook from front to back, ch1; rep from * twice more, inserting hook in next ch-3 sp on the large flower motif each time, sl st to first dc, fasten off.

Small flower motif

With colour B and 3mm hook make 6 chain and sl st to first ch to join into a ring.

Round 1 (RS): Ch1 (does not count as st), 12dc into ring, sl st to first dc to join, fasten off. (12 dc)

Round 2: Join colour A in any st with a sl st, ch1 (does not count as st), dc in each of the next 5 sts. Identify the two ch-sps on the outside of the medium flower motif that are opposite the join to the large flower motif; these will be the two spaces where you join the small flower motif. Sl st in the first of these ch-sps, inserting the hook from front to back, dc in next st on the small flower motif, sl st in the second ch-sp on the medium flower motif, dc in each remaining st on the small flower motif to end, ch30 for toe loop, sl st to first dc, fasten off.

Ankle ties

Note that the ties are joined to the flower motifs by small ring motifs, and finished with a small ring motif on each end.

Ring motifs

Make 2 of colour B and 2 of colour C for each sandal

With a 3mm hook, make 6 chain and sl st to first ch to join into a ring.

Round 1 (RS): Ch1 (does not count as st), 12dc into ring, sl st to first dc to join, fasten off.

Identify the 3 ch-sps on the top of the large flower motif that are opposite the join; you will be joining a tie in each of the first and third of these spaces.

With colour A, join with a sl st to any st of a colour C ring motif, ch8, remove hook and pass end of chain through one of the joining ch-sp on the top of the large flower motif, put hook back in loop, ch8 and sl st into the same st at base of chain on ring motif, fasten off.

Repeat with the colour B ring motif, joining in the other ch-sp on the large flower motif. Repeat with both ring motifs on the other sandal.

With a double length of colour A and 4mm (US 6) hook, join with a sl st to a st on the ring motif opposite the last join. Make a chain approx 75cm (29in) long (or desired length), sl st to another ring motif for the end of the tie. Repeat for the other tie, and do the same on the other sandal.

Fasten off and and weave in all ends.

Twinkle Toes

Put some sparkle in your step with these simple but sassy metallic sandals. These are so easy to make that the hardest part will be choosing some stunning yarns before you begin. Try something different with black and bronze, or use classic silver and gold as I have done.

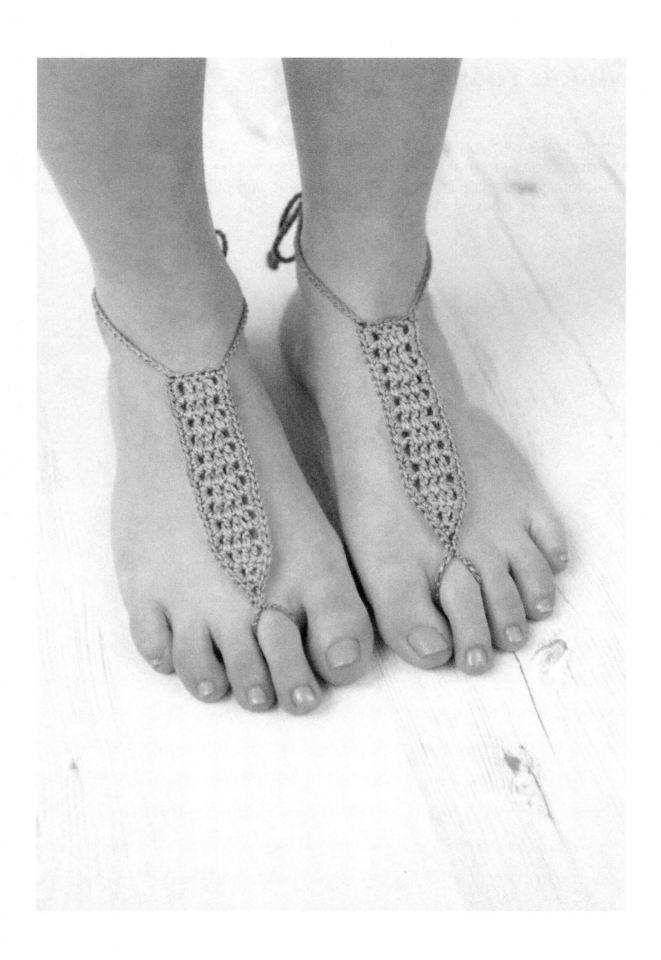

You will need

- Mercerised long-staple cotton yarn, one ball each in two colours. I used DMCPetra 3 in gold 53045 (A) and silver 5414 (B)
- Crochet hook: 2.5mm (US B/1)
- Yarn needle and scissors

Stitches used

- ✓ Chain (ch)
- ✓ Double crochet (dc)
- ✓ Treble crochet (tr)
- ✓ Slip stitch (sl st)

Metallic motif

make 2

In colour A, make 4 chain.

Row 1: 2tr in 4th ch from hook. Turn.

Row 2: 3ch (counts as tr), 1tr in same st, 1tr, 2tr in last st (top of ch3 from prev row), turn. (5tr)

Rows 3–12: 3ch (counts as tr), 4tr. Make each tr between the posts of the trebles from the previous row.

Fasten off.

> **TIP**
> The yarn I have used is washable – great for a crocheted item that you wear on your feet! It's well worth checking the care instructions on your yarn before you buy.

Edging

Hold motif with RS facing. With colour B, beginning at top left corner and working in a clockwise direction, along the long edge first, make 2dc across the stitches at the ends of each row, until you reach the pointed end.

At the point work 1dc, 17ch, sl st in 15th ch from hook (making toe-loop), 2ch, 1dc.

2dc in each st along other long edge.

Fasten off.

Block your motifs to neaten them by damping with warm water and pinning into shape until dry.

Ankle ties

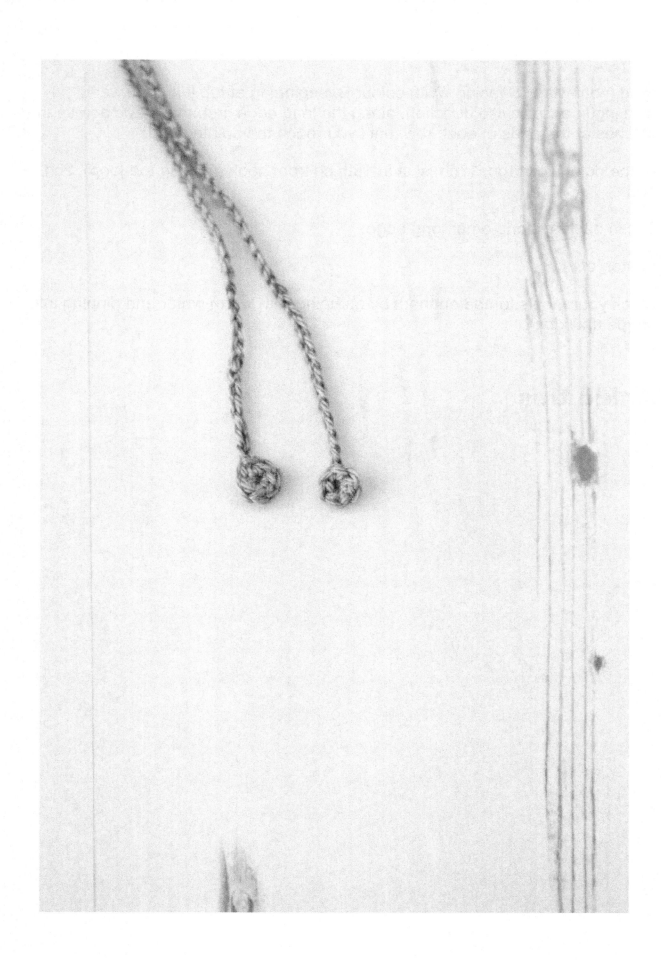

Add one to each sandal

In colour B 2ch, 6dc in 2nd st from hook, join with a sl st to first dc. Then 60ch, 5dc across top of motif, 62ch, 6dc in 2nd st from hook, join with sl st to first dc.

Fasten off, weave in ends.

Trio of Hearts

Love, love, love your feet! Show them you care by giving them three crocheted kisses in the form of these irresistible little hearts. Variegated yarn will always surprise and delight you, so choose something experimental to give these sandals some wow factor.

You will need

- 4 ply variegated mercerized cotton, 1 ball. I used Scheepjeswol Larra Batik 7501
- Crochet hook: 3mm
- Yarn needle and scissors

Stitches used

✓ Chain (ch)
✓ Double crochet (dc)
✓ Half Treble crochet (htr)
✓ Treble crochet (tr)
✓ Slip stitch (sl st)

Hearts motif

make 2

Round 1: Make 15 chain and sl st to 1st ch to form a toe loop.

Round 2: Ch7 and sl-st to 3rd ch from hook to form a loop.

Round 3: Holding the ch7 out of the way so that you can work the heart over the top of the initial chain, ch3 (counts as tr) and into the loop from the previous round work 3tr, 3htr, dc, ch1, 1 tr, ch1, dc, 3 htr, 4tr) ss into centre.

Rounds 4–7: Repeat rounds 2 and 3 twice more.

Block your motifs to neaten them by damping with warm water and pinning into shape until dry.

TIP

Because the heart motifs are not very big, chose a variegated yarn with fairly short colour changes, so that each heart contains more than one colour when it's finished.

Ankle ties

make 2

Round 1: Ch100 and fasten off.

Round 2: Attach a new piece of yarn to the top of the 3rd heart. ch100 and fasten off.

Weave in the loose ends with a darning needle.

Ivory Star Flowers

Add a touch of sophistication with these delicate pale ivory sandals. If you are lucky enough to be planning a beach wedding, or a any special summer celebration, scatter some stars on your feet and turn heads as you trip the light fantastic.

You will need

- Mercerised long-staple cotton yarn, one ball. I used DMC Petra 3 in ivory 53901
- Crochet hook: 2.5mm (US B/1)
- Yarn needle and scissors

Stitches used

- ✓ Chain (ch)
- ✓ Double crochet (dc)
- ✓ Half treble crochet (htr)
- ✓ Treble crochet (tr)
- ✓ Slip stitch (sl st)

Star flower motifs

One of the motifs incorporates the toe loop, so needs a slightly different pattern.

Star flower motif with toe loop

make 2

Round 1: Either work 6dc into a magic ring or make 2 chain and work 6dc in 2nd chain from hook. Sl st to first dc to join round. (6dc)

Round 2: 3ch, sl st into next dc. Repeat around to make 6 petals.

Rnd 3: sl st into ch3-sp. (2ch, 1tr, 16ch, sl st into 15th ch from hook (making toe loop) 1ch, 1tr, 2ch, sl st in same space), (sl st, 2ch, 1tr, 2ch, 1tr, 2ch, sl st) in each ch3-sp around.

Fasten off, weave in ends.

Remaining star flower motifs

(make 8, joining the last petal of each one to the previous flower *)

Round 1: 6dc in magic ring or make 2 chain and work 6dc in 2nd chain from hook. Sl st to first dc to join round. (6dc)

Round 2: 3ch, sl st in next dc. Repeat around to make 6 petals.

Round 3: sl st into ch3-sp. (2ch, 1tr, 2ch, 1tr, 2ch, sl st in same sp), (sl st, 2ch, 1tr, 2ch, 1tr, 2ch, sl st) in each ch3-sp around*.

*for last petal, in ch3-sp: 2ch, 1tr, 1ch. Then insert hook from front to back into ch2-sp of previous flower, yarn over and pull yarn through all loops. Then 1ch, 1tr, 2ch, sl st into same ch3-sp of original flower.

Fasten off, weave in ends.

Block your motifs to neaten them by damping with warm water and pinning into shape until dry.

TIP
Weave in the ends of yarn as you finish each star flower, rather than leaving them all to do at the end when it will become something of a chore.

Ankle ties

make 2 of each

Long tie

Starting in 2nd flower from toe loop flower, in the 3rd petal to the left (for left foot) or right (for right foot) sl st in ch2-sp.

105ch, 1dc in 2nd ch from hook, 1htr, 1tr, 1htr, 1dc, sl st.

Fasten off, weave in ends.

Short tie

Starting in last flower from toe loop flower, in the 4th petal, make sl st in ch2-sp.

135ch, 1dc in 2nd ch from hook, 1htr, 1tr, 1htr, 1dc, sl st.

Fasten off, weave in ends.

Techniques

Abbreviations
*: repeat stitches between asterisks
beg: beginning
ch: chain
ch-sp: chain space
dc: double crochet
dc2tog: double crochet two stitches together
htr half treble crochet
picot: ch3, ss into top of dc you have just made (put your hook through v-shaped stitches)
rep: repeat
RS: right side
sp: space
ss: slip stitch
st/s: stitch/es
tr: treble crochet
ttr: triple treble crochet
WS: wrong side
yrh: yarn round hook

crochet terms

Be aware that crochet terms in the US are different from those in the UK. This can be confusing as the same terms are used to refer to different stitches under each system.

The lists here give abbreviations and a translation of UK terms to US terms:

UK/US Crochet Terms	
UK term	**US term**
single crochet	slip stitch
double crochet	single crochet
half treble half	double crochet
treble	double crochet
double treble	treble crochet
treble treble	double treble crochet

The starting loop or slipknot

Before you begin, you will need to make your first stitch. This will form the basis for all the following stitches. Make a loop near the cut end of the yarn and insert the crochet hook into the loop, picking up the end of the yarn leading to the ball. Draw this new loop of yarn through the existing loop, and gently pull on the end of the yarn leading to the ball to tighten this new loop around the hook. This is your first stitch.

Crochet stitches

Chain

(abbreviation = ch)

Almost all crochet items start with a length of chain stitches, and they also often appear within stitch patterns. Wherever the chain is required, it is made in the same way.

To make a chain stitch, take the yarn over the hook, wrapping it from the back, up over the hook towards the front, and then down and under the hook (every time the yarn is taken over the hook it should be done in this way). Now draw this new loop of yarn through the loop on the hook to complete the chain stitch.

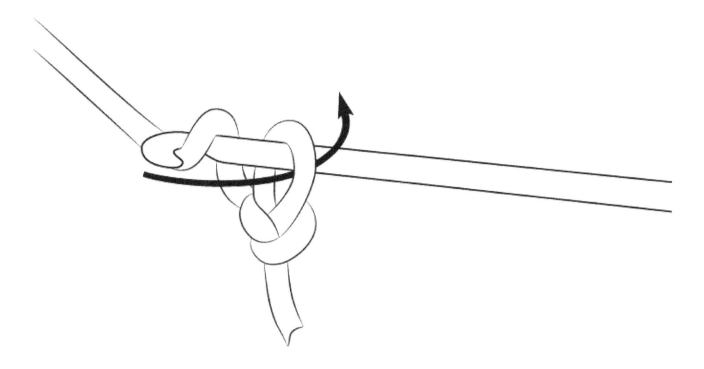

Double crochet

(abbreviation = dc)

A double crochet stitch is one of the most commonly used and easiest crochet stitches to make.

To make a double crochet, start by inserting the hook into the work at the required point. Take the yarn over the hook and draw this new loop of yarn through the loop on to the hook – there are now two loops on the hook. Take the yarn over the hook again and draw this new loop through both the loops on the hook. This completes the double crochet stitch.

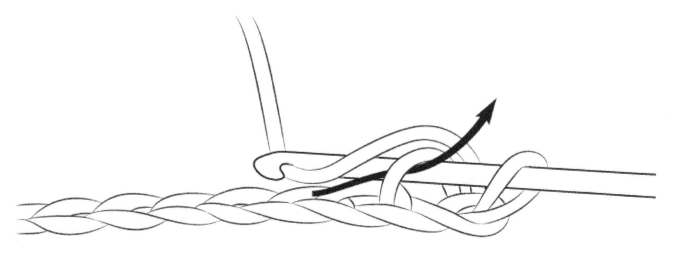

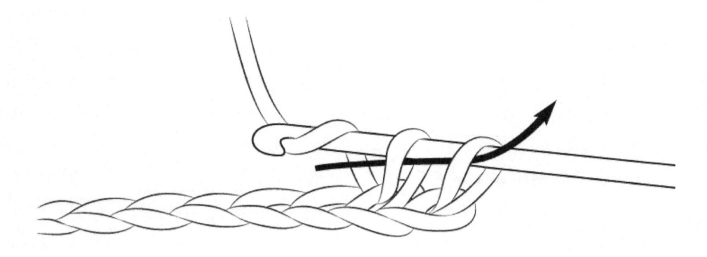

Double crochet two together

(abbreviation = dc2tog)

A double crochet two together stitch is used when you need to reduce the number of stitches you need.

To double crochet two together start by inserting the hook into the work at the required point. Take the yarn over and pull through the stitch (you will have two loops on your hook). Now insert your hook into the next stitch.

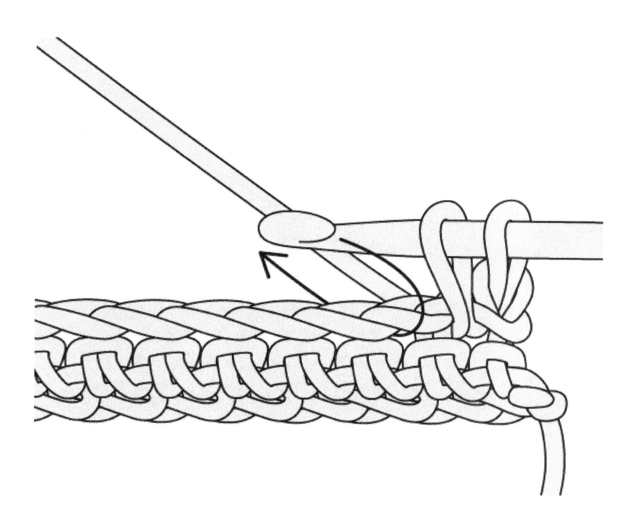

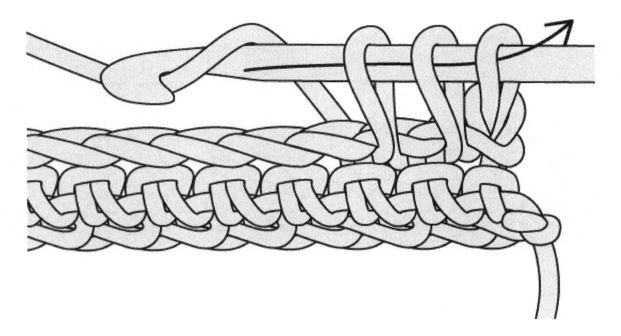

Yarn over the hook and pull yarn through the stitch (now with three loops on your hook). Yarn over hook again and pull yarn through all three loops.

Treble crochet

(abbreviation = tr)

This is the other most commonly used crochet stitch: while a double crochet stitch is a very short, compact stitch, a treble stitch is taller and will add more height to the work.

To make a treble, wrap the yarn around the hook before inserting it into the work. Wrap the yarn around the hook again and draw this loop through the work – there are now three loops on the hook.

Wrap the yarn around the hook once more and draw this new loop through just the first two loops on the hook – the original loop and this new loop.

Wrap the yarn around the hook again and draw this new loop through both loops on the hook to complete the treble stitch.

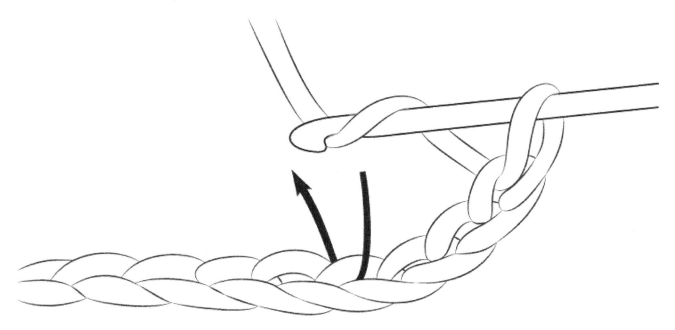

Half treble

(abbreviation = htr)

A half treble stitch is a variation of a treble; its height is halfway between that of a double crochet and a treble stitch.

To make a half treble, start in exactly the way a treble is made until there are three loops on the hook. Wrap the yarn around the hook once more and draw this new loop through all three loops on the hook to complete the half treble stitch.

Double treble

To make a double treble wrap the yarn around the hook twice, insert the hook into the next stitch, yarn over again and pull up a loop,*yrh and pull through 2 loops repeat ** 2 more times to complete stitch.

Slip stitch

(abbreviation = ss)

This stitch adds virtually no height to the work. It is generally used either to move the hook and working loop to a new point, or to join pieces. To make a slip stitch, insert the hook into the work at the required point. Take the yarn over the hook and draw this new loop through both the work and the loop on the hook to complete the slip stitch.

Picot stitch

(abbreviation = picot)

To make the picot stitch make three chain stitches, then slip stitch in the third chain from the hook.

Treble cluster

(abbreviation = trcl)

To make a treble cluster take your yarn over the hook, then insert the hook into the stitch, take your yarn over the hook again and draw through. Repeat the yarn over hook and draw through two loops, yarn over hook again, then insert the hook into the stitch once more. Bring the yarn over the hook again and draw through, then yarn over the hook again and draw through two loops. Take your yarn over the hook one last time and draw it through the remaining three loops on the hook.

Basic techniques

Joining new colours

When you're about to change colours, work until there are two loops left on your hook. Leaving a tail, draw the end of the new colour through the two loops on the hook.

Continue in the pattern with the new ball of yarn. Once complete, weave in the tails of both colours to secure.

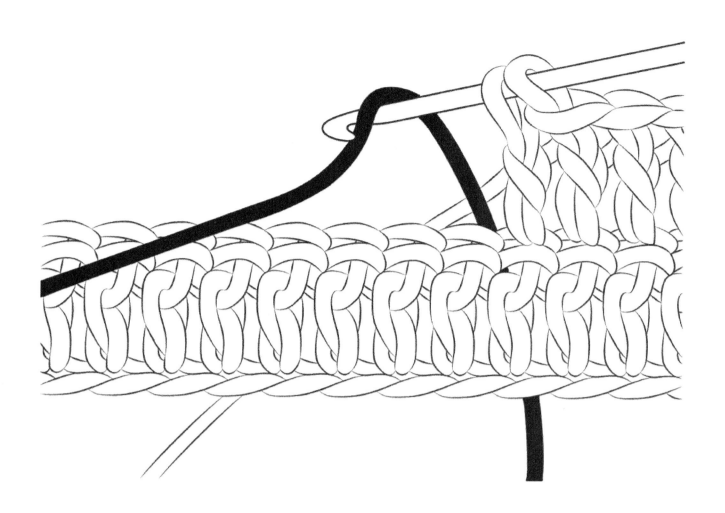

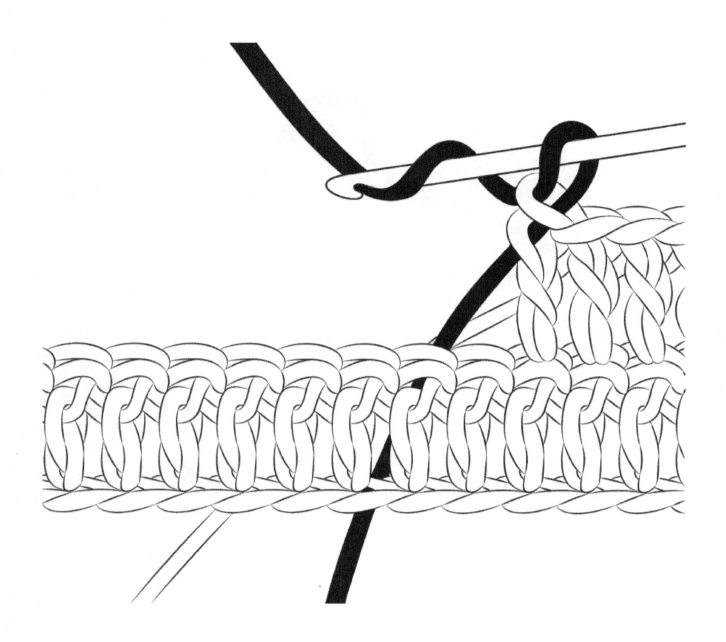

Working in the round

Sometimes, rather than working in rows, you will want to crochet in rounds. When you begin, you will need to join the foundation chain to create a ring. Make the required number of chain stitches and then use a slip stitch into the first chain to join the work.

Then, with your first round, work either into the centre of the ring as if it were a chain space, or into the chain stitches themselves as normal.

At the end of the first round of any crochet piece, the first and last stitches need to be joined together to complete the circle. This is usually done by working a slipstitch into the top of the first stitch.

To make the second and every following round of crochet, the hook must, as when working in rows, be raised up to the height of the new stitches. So each new round of crochet will start with a turning chain.

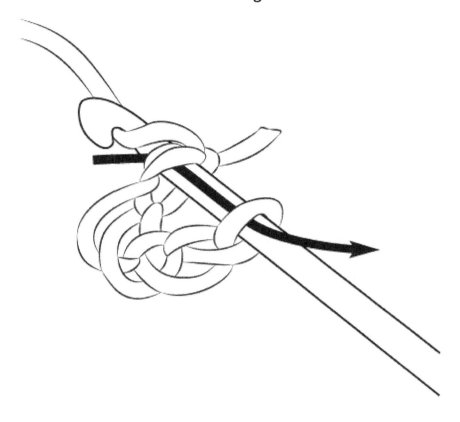

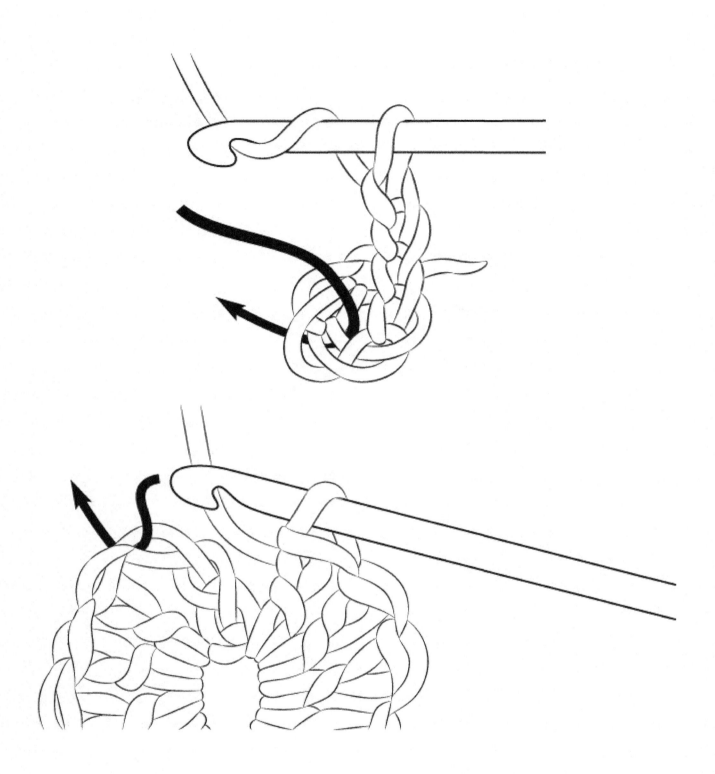

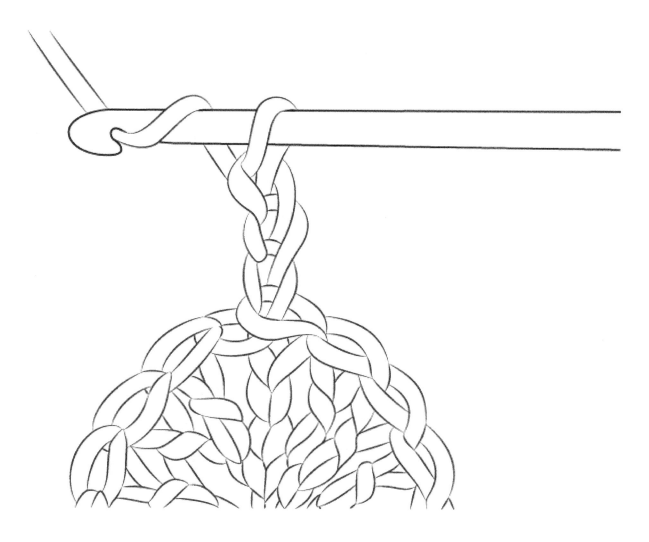

Magic ring

The magic ring is an alternative way to begin crocheting in the round. In contrast to working into a chain or a chain circle, the basic magic ring allows you to tighten the first row, eliminating any opening.

To make a magic ring, make a loop a few inches from the end of your yarn. Grasp the join of the loop (where the two strands of yarn overlap) between your left thumb and forefinger. Insert hook into the loop from front to back. Draw up a loop.

Ch 1 (does not count as st).

Insert hook into the loop, so you are crocheting over the loop and the yarn tail. Draw up a loop to begin your first sc of Round 1. Complete the sc. Continue to crochet over the loop and the yarn tail until you have the required number of sc for your first round. Grab the yarn tail and pull to draw the centre of the ring tightly closed. Begin your second round by crocheting into the first stitch of the first round.

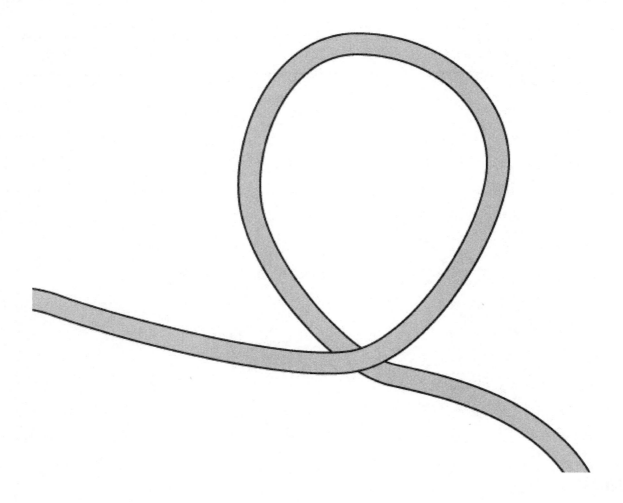

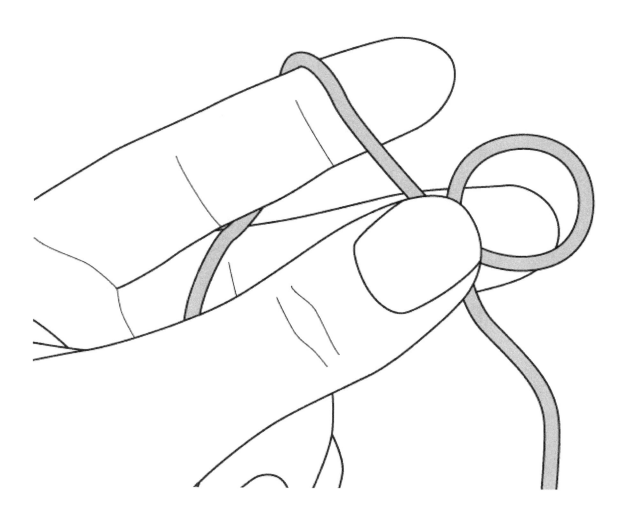

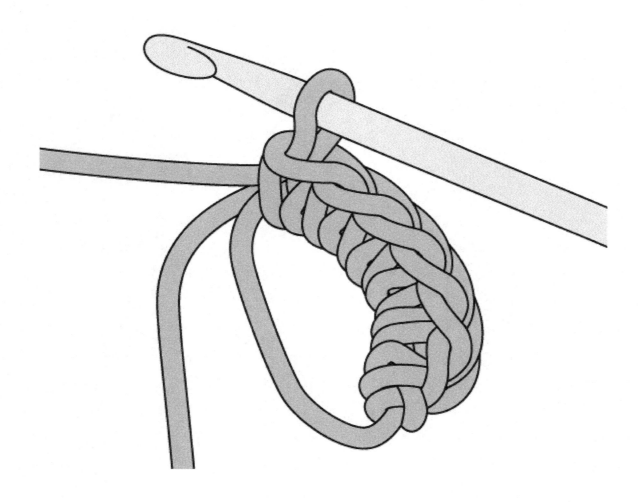

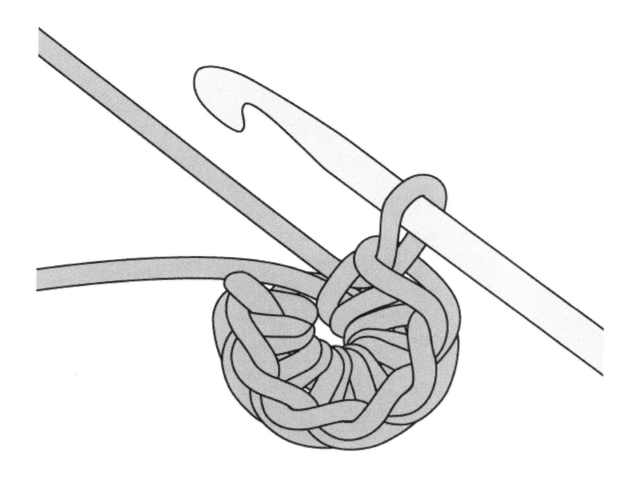

Fasten off

When you reach the end of your pattern, you will need to fasten off properly to ensure your crochet work is secure and does not unravel. This is very simple to do. You will finish with one loop on the hook. Cut the yarn, leaving a tail. Draw the tail through the loop on the hook and gently pull the yarn to tighten the stitch so that it does not unravel.

Blocking

Blocking is a technique to stop projects curling up and make them look more defined.

There are two main methods for blocking wet blocking and steam blocking. Steam blocking works better for projects made using natural yarns.

Wet blocking

You will need

- Pins
- A flat surface
- Spray bottle filled with warm water

How to wet block

1. Pin your crocheted item onto the suitable surface to the desired shape. Make sure the pins are evenly spaced around the edges and pull the crochet gently.
2. Spray, but don't soak, with warm water.
3. Leave to dry completely.

Steam blocking

You will need

- Pins
- A flat surface – an ironing board works well
- Iron with steam setting

How to steam block

1. Heat the iron to the steam setting.
2. Shape and pin the crochet onto the surface.
3. Hold the iron above your work, releasing steam evenly across the surface.
4. Leave to dry.

Printed in Great Britain
by Amazon

39417435R00066